Dedicated to those who s

can conspire with; racism, colonialism, ...

homophobia and others.

To my parents, thank you for your love and wisdom. To the

pastors, missionaries, mentors, professors and spiritual

directors who spent countless hours loving and mentoring

me. You are good people. There are billions of other good

people in the world who think differently, and we need to

get better at loving them.

Thank you to all the people who stayed in my life, even

though we didn't agree. To the stones in my shoe that

made me slow down—enough to figure out I was

running on quicksand.

INTRODUCTION

Hi, my name is Timothy. I'm a recovering Christian. This book is about my journey to process the pain of misguided faith. It is pretty goddamn traumatizing to realize that every special area of magic in your life, which you thought was a gift from God, actually just felt special because you were too stupid to know that God didn't exist. Writing this book at least, helped me. Or maybe that's just how patriarchal men process emotion, by inventing gods (or poetry books), and selling them for profit.

As a white male I am the "apex predator" of systems which Christianity conspired with in its rise to dominance (such as patriarchy and racism). My own neuroticism and laziness allowed me to create a complex web of lies around spirituality. Those lies created a comfortable bubble that kept me from seeing the harm that their associated systems did against beautiful Indigenous communities, special LGBTQ2S+ souls, and women to name a few. For that, I apologize. This book is just a start. It'll take a lifetime to rewrite my mental habits; but I'm committed to the journey.

There are many virtues to Christianity, but it's not my place to discuss them. There are far too many alive who have suffered from it more than me. I can say that what inspires me most about the Bible is its radicalism. In its day it was the stuff of revolution. Some broke, low-income, pseudo-feminist carpenter changed the course of history.

This book starts with a few of the poems I wrote when Christianity was my world. I also remember the time and place when it fell apart for me. I "de-converted," and the faith I had identified with vanished. You might catch the clue identifying which poem marked my shift from being a Theist, to something of an Ignostic.

Eventually, I found hope again. Even if hope is just a neurological ploy to balance our anxious amygdala; it is real. Its tenacious existence gives me a deep spiritual mysticism as I walk through this beautiful world. Even if I'm just a simple nerd attempting poems, creations and community to make our planet better; because life is frickin awesome and worth fighting for.

15 years ago I thought rock music was evil. 10 years ago I thought the planet was 6,000 years old. 5 years ago I thought that climate change wasn't real and that marginalized minorities were just lazy. 2 years ago I thought economists knew what they were doing. 1 year ago I thought I knew how to work. I will probably discover I'm wrong again.

It's a messy world with messy problems, but thankfully it's full of authentic people. Life takes hard work digging into the complexity of science with a curiosity that is always questioning itself. Thankfully, we can find incredible people along the way. They can make failures the stuff of laughter (beer certainly helps). Perhaps we could do that together sometime? I'll bring the beer (you did buy the book after all).

P.S. The artwork was done by a friend.

The Gist:

My faith is beautiful,
but something isn't right.

God, please exist.
But not like they say.

What just happened?
Wait, before you go!

(I can't do) life from scratch.
Oh, hello again.

"I look to You for rest

I find in You true peace

My life is a word of Your grace

May I wake in seeing Your face"

MY FAITH IS BEAUTIFUL

Arms of Marigold

Whispers are hushed by a muffled sob,
We gasp to grapple with such sudden loss.
Eyes rise with love for the wailing ones.
Before me is a coffin, draped in simple white.
Weeping from a daughter, mourning from a wife.
Cry out O shocked daughter, wail louder loving wife!
You just carried your failing beloved to medical help,
And before you thought the care had even started,
His heart had stopped.

Brother, this morning you spoke with him your last.
He would have seen your son's graduation,
But in tragedy's shadow, all thought of joy is past.

Upon the simple white there rests a simple cross,
He loved God, loved others and pointed up to Christ.
What shock is now his passing, how bitter now the knife;
We saw him just this morning joyous, full of life.
In minor melody the words cut through,
"On clouds we tread, In Christ we can ascend"
In front a voice forces out the song with strength.
Climbing upon those words,
while tears fall down her cheeks.

The cross, it is of marigolds, of beauty, of life.
The arms they are not flat but draping down,
around an empty shape
Cry out O daughter, wail loving wife
Your tears are not forgotten,
Rajendra sees with tearful face
Enwrapped in arms of marigold,
his master's warm embrace

From Good Friday Service

It was all dark
There was, broken heart.
A mother weeping for her son.
A crowd not knowing what they had done.

Soldiers jeering.
Satan cheering.
And I was silent in it all.

The man had cried.
God had died.
On the day of all blackness

Rumble and chatter.
Ripple through all matter.
As creator became savior.
Death and darkness shattered.

Love is Never Wasted

Love is never wasted,
like a seed upon dry ground
It never has no goodness
it's a treasure where it's found
Yes you can be wrong,
and yes you will make some mistakes
But you can't be blaming love
for what the evil takes

Wasted love is love

that never ever was

Hating love is loving hate,

hating just because

Selfish love is love that kills,

felt it was owed reward

Such love deserves no special song,

no ballad to record

True love shines like a beacon,

an unprotected grin

As it goes out gleaming,

it shines hope back deep within

Love is not a drink that you

can pour out and be done

Love can be refilled

when you know you're not the one

Love was once poured out, in such a torrent,

such a storm

The actor had no reason,

but the hope it would transform

If ever love was wasted,

then it was upon a cross

Our life is tied up in that tale,

was that love a loss?

Love is a deposit into others,

into you

It changes and it stretches,

till you wish that you were through

Your heart can be expanded

when it's captured by above

Safe will be your wounded soul

and guarded be that love

Roots In Years

These roots go down for a thousand years
I hear the lies, I have such fears.
My whole life's in grime,
It's the end of time.
All that's left is drink and bitter tears

These roots go down for a thousand years.
In a world that cries, with a pain that sheers.
Can't there be some hope?
As we blindly grope.
All we thought would save left us grinding gears.

These roots go down for a thousand years.
Has there been a word from a God who hears?
Could touch a cross?
Could God suffer loss?
Letting love gush out when poked by spears.

These roots go down for a thousand years
Tell me the lies tell me your fears
The end of time,
it's the opening rhyme,
take life to fight on through the tears

P.S. 10

Moonshot

Oh God help us
For we are at war
Our fear has divided us
It has torn us apart
We can't find inside us
The grace that we need
To combine and guide us
And save us from greed

So we shoot for the moon

Oh God help us
Death is always at our door
One missed pulse between us
And the mystery in store
We cannot see before us
Tomorrow will not rhyme
We need your eyes beside us
As we make steps today

So we shoot for the moon

Oh God help us

For there is war within

To feed the beast that is us

Our passion is our fire

It burns red hot inside us

And it burns us up inside

Our lust will fast destroy us

And if not our guilt will kill

So we shoot for the moon

Oh God help us

Help us reach the stars

Bring our questions to your answers

Land our hearts upon your hand

Guide us in the pastures

Where we will find peace of soul

All we have is hope you're listening

Our dream is that you're real

So we grasp at the night sky waiting

Waiting, and watching the moon

© Timothy Lipp

P.S. 12

How do I know God Exists?

The world is a waterfall of broken tears and wasted years.
If our parents have been good then it has taken us a long to
come to this realization.
Tragedy is at the root of ruined childhoods.
But as our mind and soul begins to mature it's healthy to
understand how everything burns.
How corruption is at the peak of political power.
How starvation is the norm for millions
of people just like you.
How the wealth and blessings you hold are bolstered up by
wickedness of the past.
There is much more pain than the greatest cynic
has ever known.
And in such a place those who are blind will remain.
Strangely this is where humankind finds safety.
In the walls of negativity.
In the castles called realism.
In the propaganda we call news.
In the hollow spell of being informed.
This is not good.
We have made the heart of evil our very home.

But there is amazing news to be told.

The darkness is coldest before the dawn.

The lion fights the hardest just before it falls.

Deception wins.

And suddenly it loses forever.

Life comes from pain only because pain is on its way to
death.

Those who have opened eyes.

Who reach into the world around them

and let it be their guide.

Who are not distracted by the

crashing collapse around them.

Realize that the collapse is just the crumble of a cell that we
thought was our home.

If you would like to to see how the world is getting better.

Take note of how many people will want

to take you off the way.

Nothing will be more a lie

Why is it that joy is more painful than pain?

Why does it hurt more, seem less expected, to be

outrageously enamoured with life?

That's how I feel. My fight for life has never been happier.

*elle

bloom, soft blow
butterfly in my palm
rest, be at peace
or fly, take no shame
only to defend
does love clench

Sword Drill

A two edged sword without any handle
The firmer your grasp, the deeper it wounds you
In raising this blade to cut at your brother
Your heart too must bleed, in love for the other

Curt Crack

There is a crack in my heart, a wound in its deepest part.

A scar of a battle, oh how old was its start!

Each day that I'm walking,

each footstep I tread,

it's always with me, always ahead.

If you give me your hand, then I'll guide it to the spot.

Your finger could feel the tremor, of my most anxious

thought --

The raw depth of horror, in the evils I've sought.

Maybe that sight will cause you revolt,

and a gasp and a hatred,

at what's under this molt.

If it does, then that's fine.

The shame is all mine.

But maybe,

just maybe,

We need not unwind.

Can we sit here in silence, before this raw place?

And speak of a solace, anoint it with grace?

We know that our words are just ripples in space--

but maybe our sharing, the pain will replace.

Maybe, just maybe, in the sharing of hurting, small healing

we'll taste.

Divine Marksman

You spoke not to my greatness,
to my strength or might or will,
not to all I think is powerful—
not to my wisdom or my skill.

But to what is broken.
There.
There, you have spoken.

Words rose like arrows high in the sky.
From a hand that is hidden—far to fly.
They hit their place—I start to cry.

For hidden too was their target.
Though I tried to conceal,
the arrows have marked it.
The pain has rekindled a touch I'd lost to care.
A fire that is burning with a touch that God is there.

If there is a way past all my fears,
then that way that was hidden—
washes open with tears.

BUT SOMETHING ISN'T RIGHT

Shivers

I've got shivers in my soul, whimpers in my heart.
Aches that just keep hurting, tearing me apart.
Wounds that keep on bleeding,
from a wound that's hard to find.
Maybe I'm onto something—or maybe—
I've lost my mind.

I think that they're a message saying
there is so much more.
More than all this brokenness, hate and pain and war.
Hope in all the trials, saying one day they'll be past.
Answers to the questions, something that'll last.

This pain could be the only thread,
that ties to what's real.
Even that could be beautiful, to have some stronger seal

But something's truly broken, when pain is the only voice,
All that can speak to true, the guide in every choice.

If there is indeed a word in the beauty all around,
Maybe it's a whisper that the truth is underground.

P.S. 19

Song to Judgement

The chords are building, in the infinite song.

The notes sometimes shrilling, yet guided along.

Each person a placement, with a part, with a beat.

Their hearts have a rhythm which grows as they meet.

The song somehow seems, so difficult to hear.

If anything, a caucaphony, a fuge full of fear.

But there in a whisper, here in a trill.

A touch of the harmony, that's guided by skill.

Shrill is so often the sound on this ground.

Pain comes again in some heart-stopping round.

By people, by planet, by pestilence it pounds.

Where is that theme? Oh I know it must be!

It climaxed with Christmas, and onto a tree.

The ears are now many, attuned to the song.

From tribes and all cultures is building a throng.

May all hear the echoes, and the touches that flow.

Along in each sorrow, not just guiding the show.

Here comes the composer, with a beat in his chest.

A weak, simple rhythm, stopped to give us true rest.

Judgement remains only.

Only for that which love cannot transform.

Since Sinai

"Write me down, put me in a box.
Separate—from the power that talks.
Be free from the sound waves now shaking your ears,
transcribe them, contain them, and coddle your fears.
But as you parse and examine these words in a book—
You may have a substance, but the vibrance forsook.
Those words are but scratches. It's the speaker who shines,
with all wonder, passion, beauty—all—your soul mines."

Now why would our Creator, let his speech be contained?
On paper made by creatures whose hands are blood stained?
Could his message stoop so lowly to grace
our ears so shamed?
Then be written and forgotten
by the ones that he has named?

For at his words the mountain shook,
and now they're trapped up in a book,
for by his hands he healed the blind,
But—somehow now they're trapped in mine.

WTF Christians

Where is the Christ?
All I see is a mission.
A Christ-less Christian.
Not Christlike at all.

Fear has invaded,
expertly persuaded—
a wild battle cry.
As you war with the foe,
as you "truth" clearly show,
you are playing mere games—
the paths demons know.

But how is that faith?
Bitter displays,
of the enemy's ways.
Where is the insight?
Where is the wise?
Ever angst and ever anger.
ever strategies devise.

Find me somewhere.
this warring king you serve.
It's not the lamb I know,
slain, who death did not deserve.

Please just be silent.
Until you're not self-reliant.
Until the master breaks,
Your heart and takes
fear's exalted place.

Under A Rock

I am enraged at every page, tired of waiting for this all.

Tired of sitting in the midst of shallow,

tired of holding back my gall.

I'm probably piggish, probably rude,

but I'm tired of calling holy all that reeks of prude.

God give some thrills, some vein pumping fills, that blast

past this life which mere morals distills.

Why do I have such a stupid heart, that wants to feel into

the depth of each part?

Why must I burn so hard with desire, seeking so fervently

to be burned up by fire?

Does all of my passion lead to fast-fading glee, or is it only

my hurting that really sets me free?

I do love the small things, and the tidily delights,

but my lust is for all things, I want the big bites.

Just hold it.

Please shut up if all you've got is some arbitrary mantra of

what is true life,

I've already been told it.

If you would convince me,

there are two things that can pinch me.

Overwhelming compassion—to love
when it's not in fashion,
And razor sharp insight--the kind that makes the dark
burden of reality more light.
Please proceed if that's what you'd like to say.
If not I'll hear your bullshit like the sky feels the ocean's
spray.
I guess I did just swear,
It's emotional language, it shows that I care.
Yes I am selfish and my lust is my god,
but this is the skin that I live with and fight with and plod.
Sometimes I feel like my heart is a frog in a pot that's been
warming for long,
And that my nerves are just deceivers
singing some sadistic song.
But this pot is much bigger than my world or my shell,
It's the tears of other people who are with me here in hell.
"Oh they can just hop out, they can just jump"
So goes the glibly said trump.
And we live wealthy dreams, feast bursting seams,
While their pain flows on in endless reams.
Where's the end of this tunnel?
Why is my heart such a stupid loving funnel?
Oh that I could fly away--
that my eyes could cry or I could even pray.
This dragon within me,

This chameleon without,

this raging dark hailstorm,

this long-lasting drought.

I could flee to the hills,

of my pet sins and thrills.

To some porn or some youtube,

or some bad-tasting brew-tude.

But instead I'll just grumble,

and eloquently mumble.

With my fingers a typing all the sounds of my griping.

Maybe this word will be a message in a bottle,

maybe my anger can speed up the throttle--

Of the right that is riding on its way to my place,

of the peace that is waiting to rest on my face.

Bind Me

I may never arrive
I may only survive

The path on is dreary
Perhaps I am weary
Of the worries and weights that bear on the world
Of my failings and errors and judgements absurd

But I don't know why
I seem to have it all
Such wealth and allurements
I should stand so tall

But hollow disappointments are all I seem to me
They're truly just the twitching's of a devil that is free
Oh I believe,
my heart is relieved,
indeed there must be more to see.

Where is the place?

Where I'll see only grace?

Where my mind won't be blinded

And my heart oft reminded

Of the echoes of evil

In a world that is dead.

Is this all discontentment?

I haven't earned my resentment!

Will the creator of all,

Spurn my bitter call?

Am I heard?

Am I absurd?

Bind me, and blind me.

Oh true,

enthrall.

–

Is God a Traffic Cop?

Is God a traffic cop?
Is God sitting, watching cars go quickly by?
Hoping one will go too fast,
so he can ticket that wicked guy.

Is God just a long red light?
That you glare at alone on those long dark nights.

Is God the threat of wrath for your saving of time?
When you just roll along,
at that needless stop sign.
Is God just some strategic,
"most of the time" rule?
Is constant devotion a speed limit for fools?
Am I driving blind?
Should I pray or stop?
Is God hiding?
A hiding traffic cop?

Jesus Loving Atheists

Atheist was a name for the early christians,
because they didn't worship gods,
they just followed Jesus.

Their scandalous faith put them in the mouths of lions.
Their scandalous love broke Rome's strong defiance.

But now there are gods that dance in the sermons,
the emperor is in our church,
the politics and power we worship.
Is there a way to the faith and love we've somehow missed?
I wonder, and start to think, that the world needs more
atheists.

Balloon

Inhale   Exhale

There was resistance on that breath.

rubber ring

plastic purse

Pushes back on the air that's left

Inhale   Exhale

A little bubble begins to grow

A ball

A sphere

Capturing much of what I blow

Inhale   Exhale

An orb now starts to fill my view

Its color

Its curve

May be all--all that's really true

Inhale   Exhale

My lungs are now strong with inflating skill

It's bigger

It's grander

And breathing doubt for its substance is my fill

Inhale

Ex-

EXPLOSION

I have filled my gag all the way to death

I brought it to life and killed it with breath

Inhale

Inhale

Exhale

Exhale

Inhale

Inhale

Exhale

Exhale

Inhale

Inhale

Exhale

Exhale

Inhale

Exhale

Inhale

Exhale

Again now the rhythm of life takes its toll

Now freely

And stronger

My lungs take in all and give to the whole

GOD, PLEASE EXIST

God, Please Exist

Each day awakes, a flower blooming new.
Each moment passes, vanishing into blue.
The threads that tie the past to now, are whispering fibers
that barely show.
Why do I feel, as if each feeling is brand new?
I surely have passed this way before,
or is this really a fresh new door?
Rolling, tumbling, morphing, growing there.
Each moment pops and then passes into air.
Each day I realize that I have not even grasped the half
of what it means to roam this earth. Millions join daily in
this cycle of birth.
When life is over it comes to an end.
But while it is going it's a reincarnating trend.
The moments pass and then return but different in a
whirring churn.
Perhaps this is my gift of forgetting.
Or is it unique to those who've died to live again?
Is this what life and growing means?
There is one outside this wheel,
who understands the spin I feel.
His constant I am, I am, is always bringing the I am I'll be.
Time is a tumbler polishing pebbles,
tuning them to precious stones.
Death is becoming a jewel on his crown.

Rest

Is this a dance
Dare we fall entranced
By the all—
so o riddled with chance

Can we live with one rule
To love and be the fool
Unwound, undone—
our life from its spool

Or instead with sense
Live in pretense
As beasts in a cage—
ever defence

The answer.
The quest
Istherearest

Born Again

I was lying in a room

Dark

Alone

No vision

No insight

No home

Then-- there was a spark

The spark became a hand

And it brought me from the past

The hand became a man

And he taught me how to stand

His form was bright and bold

It brought to life all in its hold

And then I knew for sure I had met

The creator of all—by

the life his touch left

Though all had been black I at last now had a friend

His words, his smile, brought a luminescent glow

Each one new whisps of light in the dark to show

And as his light grew the shadows began to blend
The light and the dark
The black much less stark
The out and the in
The other came within

My friend, he must be growing!
Or maybe, it was I.
Perhaps at his touch.
Something was changing in my eye.
Because, before I really noticed
My friend slowly began to fade--
No, thats not the right word--
For it all was becoming too bright to allow for any shade.

So at last his form also disappeared.

That friend who led me so gently here.

My friend was somehow,

Forever gone.

But I am also somehow,

Now never alone.

I wonder if he was ever,

Ever really there.

The one who put love and light in all when he came.

Perhaps I had built him,

Built him with prayer.

(At times in the night I still whisper his name)

I am standing in the sky

Galaxies

Brilliance

All welcome

All beauty

All home

Imaginary Friend

You are my very best, Imaginary friend

Because you know my shit

and love me without end

Other people have such trouble

Talking to them self

They think that they are crazy

But I'm not talking

Just so I am heard

I talk because you know me best

And say things I've not heard

Who really cares if you're even there

You keep me thinking on what's next

And not on how I've sinned

Who gives a damn if someone's listening to this prayer

Because I know when I talk to you

I get better than before

Maybe I'm alright,

or maybe not,

but either way you're here

Here with you, at least us two, my ever listening friend

You are my very best imaginary friend

you are right here with me through thick and thin

And what's even more

You make me better, then I was before

Call Us Afar

We are alone.

we are very alone

we are lost in a wilderness

we have lost our home

I see it in the eyes

Of the people that I meet.

I hear it in the fears

Of the strangers on the street.

Each evening,

Is empty.

With no-one to walk.

We eat our fill,

Of laugh and dance.

When all we want is someone to talk.

Someone to speak to the sorrow we bear.

Someone to share in the weight of each care.

Someone to know, just who we are.

And love us.

and hold us.

and call us.

Afar

Sunset

So magnanimously bestowed on us
are the colours of the sky
So gratuitously they pour on us
as flamboyant brushes fly
The gradient is radiant and its hues so slightly change
But glance away and you will say, "it's now wonderfully
strange"

Unashamedly my spirit must worship
as my heart is filled with awe
Yet silently my mind must curse it
"it is but clouds I saw"

As it grows darker, the colours starker,
and my soul begins to rest
We bid farewell, to the day's last spell,
and sit pondering the west

She Wasn't Interested

Flowers grow up silently
from the roots that are below.
Their beauty is a testament
to the depths their anchors go.

Some blossoms are so dainty
that they barely survive.
Others have a strength that spreads
and makes the world come more alive.

To shine so radiantly
and yet bear stormy gales like a tree.
Life must stem from a heart that
has roots in a spirit breaking free

All spirits are born from a greater one
that gives grace we can't depose.
Sometimes God makes a special one,
Sometimes there grows A Rose.

Brother Beware

Blossoming beauties
Bosoms and all
Breasts
Voluptuous petals
Eyes.
That stir my heart to sing such songs

Strolling by
I saw you
Scrolling down
Again again
Then alas
I simply found you
By a thousand others
Strolled upon

To guard and love you
To hold you close
With my vice-grip heart
Would tear you from the sacred earth
Enscald your roots
Entomb your soul and so I
Curse this
Curse this evil of my being
Curse my patriarchal birth

P.S. 44

Blessing, Confessing

My heart is eviscerated,
for a god I thought was there
Long ago each waking thought,
I sought some sort of prayer

Blessing, confessing
Guiding all to the sky
Accepting, such comfort
that I was in his eye

And now he is dead

Well not really,
I've just been honest instead.

Been honest with myself and how I project.
A dream where I think my maker reaches down.
Into my world—showing love till I am found.

Now my heart is quivering

My soul is shivering
My whole world has lost its greatest friend
And I am flattened,
myself supplanted
How did it all come crashing to this end?

The beauty, the dreams, the wonder I saw.
I thought they were divine love reaching down
But they have left me gasping—
it is just by myself I am found

God, please exist

My Final Prayer

Come to me

Like a rushing rain storm

That brings peace from the heat of the day

First I hear it far away

A patter

A hope

Then it rushes in stronger

At last I must wish no longer

And the cool brings me rest from my way

Come to me

God, please exist

Come to me
With the same passion my hand
Would wreak on the breasts and thighs
Of the lover at last found
Oh such thrusting I would bring
With such moaning we would sing
As genuine love
Latches lips to lusting
And together we cling
Come to me

Come to me
Like this and more
Come to me
Till I thirst no more
Come to me
Oh God
Come to me
Or speak no more

God, please exist

BUT

NOT

LIKE

THEY SAY

Praise God for Apostasy

Let them leave

Let this die

Let the charlatans all cry

Let the preachers loudly grieve

As the people disbelieve

In the hope that they were sold

Sold to pews,

sold

and sold

God my Loudspeaker

God my book

That guards the answers I haven't found

God my projector

That spreads the light of my perception all around

God my sword

That cuts my foes and brings them down

God my mic

That gives my words an echo of divine sound

God my

God,

God and me are so alike

The Sacred Sin

There is a sacred sin
A lie that is my truth
Long ago I was taught
That this wickedness was unique
That my lust had a special shelf in hell's gates

My passion was yes, a really big deal,
But it was being worshiped
With the act of conceal
Now as any true idol
It's now a necklace
And I'm choked with this burden
Of virgin disgrace

I hated the flames of hell
And so I kept myself from planning sex well
Now I hate just the flame of desire
That keeps me consumed with a pulsing fire
I want to just jump in the coals
Release this small load
And realise it's nothing
To carry at all

Consolata Shrine

Are you any more
Than a wondrous chord
Resonance of the horde
That raised up the spires over my head
That rises with power as words are said
Together we fund the building of these walls
Together we sing to life
the presence of our Gods

Props Thomas

Question why, question why,
Please don't, please don't, do and die
Ask and wonder, of it all
Seek and ponder, be enthralled

If I could purr then I'd be dead,
Asking questions killed the cat they said
Catching mice would not suffice
I'd like a reason, death isn't nice

Cheap and easy are those friends
Who just seek you for their ends
Deepest of all brotherhoods
Is the one of woulds not shoulds

Dig much deeper than you know
I will greet you, where you go

Church Divination

When was Jesus colonized?

Who brought the poison that led to these lies?

I hate this mindset that is lurking in place

Hiding behind a mask of my savior's face

Jesus as a man lived in time and place and land

The people of his day,

Thought their culture was the only way

To be loved by God was to be Israeli

And to know all the laws and hopefully be a "he"

But Jesus hung out with outcasts (even women)

and worse

On the system of borders he made all out war

The lines were all shunned

As love, hate outgunned

Then for some reason his countrymen killed him

I guess his message of compassion never thrilled them

But by his life after death his followers were inspired

They shook up an empire with grace that never tired

The Apostle Paul penned these words to the Ephesians

"Jesus--- broke down all the walls once between us"

So I wonder if Jesus went mental

when he saw his church build schools residential

when he saw his people love an economy

that's centered on what we can dominate

though the apostles said what is seen lasts short

we quickly forgot and built us a whole bunch of forts

Then defended our safety

With policies of hatred

Acts to solve a problem that wasn't one

A problem we'd invented and our selfishness had done

I don't blame a single church or denomination

For the horrors that happened in this nation

But I blame a single greedy definition

of what is beautiful, a narrowing vision

It wasn't the evil of one party or side

But a craving for conquering and thus to divide

If you're like me you may have felt frustrated when you see

this topic in news

Yes there is hurt that's been caused but that was back then

and those are not my views

I never pushed someone from their lands

Why should there be guilt on my hands?

But I do have a beautiful home,

and the freedom to write poems,

all things that were stolen in country I call my own

In Calgary it was taken from Blackfoot,

Siksika, and other treaty 7 nations

So since I am part of this broken promise, I will honour this

as their land without reservations

If the church has a place in truth and reconciliation

Then we have to abandon, our colonial divination

If we have a master who truly teaches compassion

We need to feel with those in pain,

and support them by action

Action to: eliminate education and employment gaps

Action to: repudiate doctrines of discovery and other legal

traps

Action to: encourage cultural and language education for

indigenous youth

Action to: critique the history

we teach as a white-washed version of the truth

These are just a few of the steps listed by the Truth and

reconciliation commission

And Words have already gone on too long,

they have just painted a vision

If there is a spark of life in this faith that we claim

Then make it real,

Make compassion revealed,

Or call it something else and forget Jesus's name.

If You Asked me to Pray

If you asked me to pray today
Then I probably would
And this is what I'd say

God help us not believe in you
Help us lose our faith
For our doctrines are just clever idols
That helps keep light on the face
Jesus keep our hearts shut to you
For this you is a lie from the devil
That is just like the person we wanted
And not like the rabbi so true
Spirit move away from us
For your passion is nothing but neurons and sparks
It's blinded us from the world as it is
And wrote a lie that God is now near

I'd pray with all the hope I have
And you would hate me still
For my eyes see what yours hate to bear
And your fear prefers to kill

© Tim Lipp

Nietsche

If God is dead,

Then let it be

And do not work so hard to build him

For oh,

If it were so,

That we had strength enough to kill him

I Live in a Big House?

I live in a big house, I haven't been to all the rooms.

Bring your box into this house, I'll put it on a special shelf.

If you happen to walk out of it one day, mind your step.

Grace of God's Absence

Heartache for heartache
Broken for broken
Death for death
Chaos for chaos
Weakness is perfectly good for it is perfectly shareable
All that we are is not condemned
All that we are is not condoned
And thus we are all blessed

Chaos has its solace in chaotic answers
And capricious suffering capriciously comforts
For we cannot blame ourselves at its advent

Our smallness makes us flounder
Our smallness cleanses our hands
God gives us the grace of his absence
As he is not here to help us
He also is not here to condemn

P.S. 62

Fistful

I grasp with my firm grip
the rope hanging there
I grasp to slow my falling,
grasp with a prayer
I grasp my fists clenched tight,
knuckles white,
For oh am I scared

I grasp,
but I keep falling,
for my hands hold naught but air

At least my hands are warm
And so my grip goes on
Though I may fall—I have my fists
And they make me feel strong

WHAT
HAVE
I
DONE?

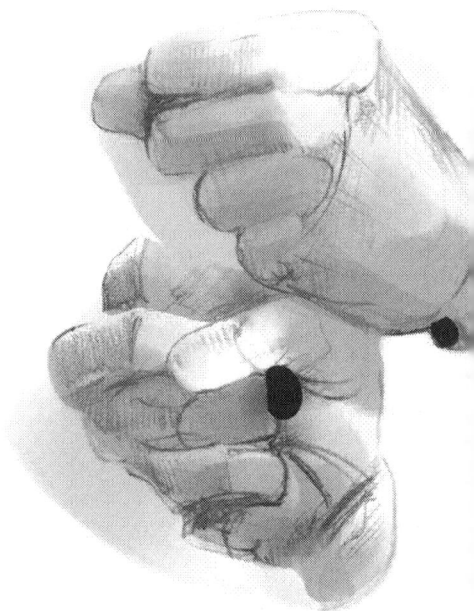

You Don't Just Say "I Don't Believe"

You don't just say
I don't believe in God anymore
Like you say
"The rain has stopped outside"
or, "let's go buy some shoes."

You say it like the words
"I want a divorce"
To your wife of 20 years.

Like the words,
"I didn't sleep alone last night"
To your partner's tears.

You don't just say it
And walk goodbye
As your world crashes down
And you wonder
Is it worth it
To shake the lie that was your crown.

Maybe those words
are like the days
A doctor gives you left to live
Every part of who you are
Is wrapped up in their quivering waves
And broken as they're said.

You don't just say
"I don't believe in God anymore"
Only their breath
is what's cavalier
They take all that you had to give
They take all that you held to live

(+/-)

The mind is an engine that driveth us insane
It fires and it moveth so fast that we learn only pain
The heart is a razor blade that cutteth us to our core
It is violent and gives no rest ever hungering for more
The spirit is our only salve, though I protest it's even there
I'll pray it is, and rest myself yonder, lest I cease to care

I'm Free

I am a boat in a sea
I am a small boat in a very large sea
I am a boat that once had chains on me
I cut them off and now I'm free

I have no chains,
oh yes I'm free
I'm free of the weight
Free of the anchor
And this,
This is a wild sea

These winds
They are blowing
They are filling a sail
My tears
They are flowing
They are guiding my trail

I did not Imagine
That I had been marooned
Till my heart started moving
And I felt this wound

I was doodling
In a dooldrum
Passionless, still.
A gale started wailing
And it started to fill
A sail I'd forgotten--
no, hidden, at will

--

Oh curse this storm
That has started to form
It has torn off my anchor

P.S. 70

It has pierced to my soul

It has broken my moorings

I am losing control

If my mind was less open

If I could play the fool

Then I wouldn't see all this broken

I could actually rule

But I'm stupidly smart

And I can see my part

In the horrors all around

As the ache and pain abound

If my heart has really moved me

Though the lies of comfort soothe me

Then I must sail and ride this sea.

Yes, though I may fail, I'll ride it free.

I must ride.

This wild sea

Plank

I am wandering onto a plank
Over the depths of a chasm with sharks
If I slip I will fall into the pain of heartbreak

Each step must be a journey into the heart of God above
Or I will turn around and flee
I will never, ever, love

Be Something

If ever there was something
Then I will stay this course
It was that heart that brought me here
There's nowhere I can hide
It's better to be hot or cold
Then mellow in my sin
So I will keep on waltzing on
In step with hot rhythm

If ever there was something
Then I cannot hide
I'm small and weak and just a man
How could my choices chide
My sin is just something
If I'm more than man
Isn't that just pride?

Cold Love

I don't ask for much anymore
I don't think you're listening so I fight my own war
But just one thing I'll ask
I ask on a prayer and a sliver of chance
Don't let my love grow cold

I wake every morning
To battle through the day
I strive with living and seek success--
but I'll probably waste it anyway
If my love grows cold

I lie in my bed
Thoughts racing in my head
My dreams seduce me and wake me again
They call to my passion
Say I'm missing on the score
So maybe I'll skip the noble path
And let my love grow cold

P.S. 74

As I slowly round the corner
I turn the final bend
I'll still live on to pleasure's song
Because somewhere there, there is something I feel
Unlike my love now cold

These could be the last words I write
My soul has reached its end
If I may be so bold...

Love is Just the Name

Love is just the name
For the magic
from which we came
It has no special trait
No divine cause
No certain fate

It's just the air we breathe
As social beings
Who care and grieve
It's just the water we drink
And survive upon
And want to sink

It's simply nothing more
than all we have
To win survival's war
And if we cut it from ourselves
We will have strength
And nothing else

Umbilical Cord

Sometimes I go back
To the world I know so well
The womb in which my hands were formed
The first time I really fell
In love
In hope
In trust
Indeed
My everything wrapped up inside
Wrapped up within belief

They say it takes eleven tries
For an abused woman to leave her curse
But I have tried a million times
And keep coming back to your words
But my umbilical cord
May never be cut
And maybe that's not for the worst
But pray as I may
What ever they say
It no longer quenches my thirst

Solace

I have neither found
In faith
Or in leaving faith itself
The deep solace
For which my soul longs

Love Divine

I followed love

O my God

The love I learned from you

Imagine the pain

Surprise and shame

To find that it

It was what birthed you

Sky God

We didn't even know
How alone we were
The echoes of our cries
Gave us comfort from afar
The sky was the limit
So above it was the cause
But why this deadly silence?
Why no words at all?
Perhaps it was our actions
That had driven God away
Or some malignant power
Standing in the way
Then as our Babels mounted
Eyes rose above the veil
And saw just how empty
The all was and we--alone
If God is somewhere out there
Perhaps he is in retreat
Or perhaps he thinks to keep us growing
Our hands must never meet

Her

Her Smile

Sends laughter

from the corners

of her eyes

The room

at once

is brighter

and peace

is at my side

the glance

has danced

my hopes up high

But I

can't catch it

even one more time

Atheist's Carol

As with the time, the seasons change
Changed evermore, have I
Now died has all I thought was real
Bye bye luli-lulay

Where once I saw, a hand in all
Now I see it was mine
Alone in death,
Mere mortal breath
Bye bye luli-lulay

All that once was, it still shall be
Only the lies shall pass
The world spins on
And love's not gone
Bye bye luli-lulay

Luli-lulay, Oh little tiny child, bye bye luli-lulay

Now that you're gone

My everything, my life, my all
It was at your beck and call
Fears and insecurities
You powerfully drove away
　　　　　I wonder if they'll be back
　　　　　　　　Now that you're gone

I had no other reason
Why I should dance or sing
I had such strength from believing
And it brought life to everything
　　　　　I wonder if I'll die
　　　　　　　　Now that you're gone

There was such hope to try
The impossible never left undone
Miracles jumped to happen
My work dreams to fashion
　　　　　Will it all be nothing but dust
　　　　　　　　Now that you're gone

When I found your words inside me
I found they were like nothing else
They bubbled up and inspired me
Poems came flying off the shelf
                    So will I drown in silence?
                              Now that you're gone

Love became less a word
As your story invaded my thoughts
All over the world love becomes a verb
As the greatest command you taught
                    Is love just a scream at death?
                              Now that you're gone

            The one who chased my fears is flied
            The hope that brought me good has died
            The spring of all my words has dried
            The source of all my love was lies

            ...

P.S. 84

Maybe you are just in my head
But you're still good and guide me on
Even if I made you all along
Why not pray to my inner God
You still feel closer now...
Now that you're gone

I do Not Hate the Light

I do not hate the light
But if I look at that incessant bright
When I gaze upon that glare
All the beauty loses fare
And awash, alas
The world is lost
In a single,
blinded
stare

To study God is stupid
As it is to stare at the sun.
But turn away
Spend each day
Studying beauty light that has won

WAIT, BEFORE YOU GO

Seasick Friendship

I spin myself dizzy
When I think of how I've changed
How do people do it
Who always stay the same

I'm sure my friends got seasick too
Cause they left me from this ride
Somehow I'm something dangerous
That makes them puke inside

P.S. 88

Tears

I tell you a story
I wrap it in tears
It is a tale of my passing
How I died through the years

I have lost my faith
I have lost my world
It died one day along my way
Yes. That's what you heard.

I came to a place
Oh I weep that I'm here
Where I see it was myself
That made the divine feel near

I dare not worship only me
For that would not be sane
So I lose my faith in the God I've formed
And find a well of pain

One comfort I have
As I drown in this noise
No true maker would seek
Any other choice

I Have Not Lost My Faith

I have not lost my faith
I have only gained more life
More wisdom, more insight
More wonder, more love
For this is my Father's world

So if you think I'm broken
Or blinded or left behind
Then yours is a God not big enough
smaller than the constructs of your mind
Who only works when you say so

I have not lost my faith
But I have gained the world
And it's so much bigger than my old man

Dearly Beloved

You are warm you are welcome in this place that you know
There are walls there are windows they protect, say it's so
Like a turtle with its armour you would never have fear
You're protected, you're defended--as long as you stay here

You sure love this place, that you know so well.

YOU ARE NOT IN A SHELL!
Oh my rage, you're in a cage‼
Why oh why can't you tell?

Grab this lifeline, please take a hold
I pass you my love, please cling, be bold.

Zits

Aren't they great?
"But I'm trying to tell myself, that it's okay.
I don't know how to hug my soul, but I'll hold
my head in my hands, and my eyes looking down.
Because I am dark, and evil inside
I am a broken, sinful person
A rebel, an outcast, a villain against all that's good
Like Lex Luthor,
except I'm also stupid and poor
The heroes are the people that lock me away
From myself and the darkness at my core."

So I went balls deep into Christianity,
But it didn't mean i would end up more like christ.
I was sold a currency that traded guilt and shame for hymns
and prayers.
Invest in the church so you will get back dividends of shame
and guilt

The zits who put you down,
have options on your fall
Because they are afraid of who they are
They want you to help them hide it too

Love yourself more,
and maybe them
Love too much to waste time
hiding from yourself

Take your hands off your face
Stop hiding yourself
If the universe let you be born
It can handle what it made
Stop giving the zits your face

Yeah Tim,
I'm talking to you

Old Mentors

How long will I carry you

Shadows of my past

Scorn never forgotten

Of old friends who never last

Your words are still the ringing

That echoes in in my ear

The shrill and scarring whisper

"Do you have no fear?"

"Why are you still here?"

To cast far off your burden

I may cast you far away

I may hate your actual being

For what the whispers say

Emergency Exit

There are little exit doors hidden well inside these words.
Were they left for me by devils
to make me go absurd?
Am I walking now by whispers
on a way to make me wild?
As they're stealing, killing, 'stroying
what was once a little child?

Or is my path so narrow it was hidden in great minds--
Of the people who were writing down
these words now thought divine?
Their subconscious sought the whole
so they left me holes to find.
And as I'm slipping through them,
I hear cheering from behind.

P.S. 96

The Banshees

The screams that haunt me,
are two, my friend.
They are two and come,
From such different ends.

From the pain and the heartache--
The world's bitter throb.
The knife as my heart breaks--
From the fear that is God.
Shattered and stolen,
Are the skies of their light.
Battered and swollen
Are we all in this night.

But with equal clamour
There is juxtaposed
An exultant hallelujah
In the world as it grows
I can't but be gasping
As the world crashes down
With a weight of such beauty
My soul is being drowned.

A song that would take me,

to heaven's great hall

A breeze is seducing,

me with a fresh call.

I wail with these banshees

And their dueling notes

For I can't see their balance

Between them I'm choked

And so to you,

My friend I must be

The endless shrieking,

of a soul in a scree.

I would that I could silence

The dissonance that I bear

But maybe it must be spoken

Maybe, I must share.

Luke 4:24

"I used to live my life
Striving so hard each day
Just to be a little more the hero
But now I have learned
Through toil and tears
Do true good and they'll call you the villain"

- Jesus

An Epitaph

He was so good.
At seeing all the bad
He helped them all forget their dreams
To dwell on what they had

"Closed and dancing were our eyes
And full of imagined fare
Then he cut us from those chains
And the world was open, bare

The safety that we held so close
Our refuge all life long
He deftly took it all away
He showed us we were wrong"

So now their lies have disappeared
But also gone is that "great" man
Who so well helped them lose it all
For the gift of empty hands

Whisp

I am but a shadow, a whisp in your world.
Just a dance, in a flag, that is never unfurled.

I walk through the world with a flutter and a fly
I leave nothing good behind but a wall of hard goodbyes

In seeking greater union in the world all around
I have left all but leaving and only parting found

I am but a shadow, but a whisp in your world
Wave your hand and I am gone, alone and absurd

Vessel

Will you let me build a vessel
For my love of this strange world
And kiss on it a blessing
With words as yet unheard

Expose my weakened heart
The vein that feeds my soul
To you my friend, to know me so
And yet still hold me close

Our love to be a chalice
For hope as yet to share
And fire, within our bosom
To offer others care

Then rise dear one
And break the broken mold
For once it's done
I'll find more love my friend

In His Own Town

I should have never tried
To manage the way you feel
My brother,
my enemy,
my friend
Humans are far too fickle
A bundle of petty emotions
To be managed at all
If even mine
Then definitely yours
So now I'm shaking my fist at God
For making us what we are
And for not making us at all
Because he doesn't exist
Of course I'm going to burn out
Trying
To fill his shoes

Curves

I look at the mountains

Curves I wish to climb

I look upon your silouette

Curves I would entwine

Both are wonders out of reach

Both are beuaties that remind

I am small,

I am weak

And the world is greater in my eyes

Then I shall ever be

Nightclub

The deepest well of lies
That the world has ever known
Was drilled when humans first were born
Upon this cursed stone
And now they echo
With the pulse of every nightclub beat
And in the words of judgement—
preached on those sinners' moving feet

Life from Scratch

IS

Does is need an explanation
Must every how become a why
Should every mystery have a reason
And every action have an I

Are we killing the wonder of the world that exists
When we force it to have a creator that fits
And in forcing, thus raping,
the divine with our mind
Ourselves just creating,
a world we can bind

Wouldn't real worship look more like a nap?
To enjoy and admire all that's transpired
Taking rest from conniving a cause for it all
Feasting.
Inviting,
a real outside call

Solomon's Wisdom

Here my child
I give you a gift
A wonder, a treasure,
None other has lived
It will be your saviour
Guide every thought
The doctrine to lead you
The comfort you sought
Hold it close to your heart
And firm in your hand
But do not make it forever yours

For insight is a gift that must be lost once it is found
And clarity of description is not clarity most profound

When you grasp how this world works
You've come upon a gem
But oh my child, let go of it,
So you may grow again

P.S. 108

Monkey On a Rock

I'm an addict
Of a curious kind
I like something sinister
That most don't mind
But when I come to a moment
Where I've done something wrong
I'll flirt and start my addiction
And in a moment I'm gone

Refrain:
Guilty me, oh guilty me
My guilt makes me happy,
It makes me feel free
I'm not just some monkey
Here on a rock
I have power over nature
My mistakes mean a lot

When I'm down on myself
I'm at the top of my list
I'm number one in my thoughts
Though I act like I'm pissed
I keep control of this problem
By thinking it's all mine
Yes I'm the boss of everything
So I'll feel guilty all the time

Refrain

You know our brains play these tricks on us
Where feeling bad feels good
We don't want to be caught doing nothing
So we dwell on what we could
But the brain's just a blob
Of grey stuff in your skull
Simply learn from your mistakes
Then move onward in doing well

Refrain

P.S. 110

A Perfect World

There is no mismatch

Between what is and could have been

No secret hand of Satan

To take and to demean

Injustice has its balance

In the chaos we all feel

So shed divine condemnation;

It is nothing real

What We Are

What we are
Be at peace
Be at peace
With what we are

From the buildings
To the playground
Always striving
Never far

Up above
Wealth and pomp
Down below
Mud and romp

What we are
Be at peace
Be at peace
With what we are

Love is Ever Wasted

I didn't believe in black holes
I thought they were just a lie
A trick invented by Christians
To keep the youth in line

But then I crossed the horizon
Of one living just next door
And now I think I'm falling
I don't know, what the heck for

It's probably some concotion
Of evolution going off in my head
To calm my licensious living
And settle down instead

It's really hard to tell
Like all the light's been pulled away
Oh I'm definitely blinded
And I secretly want the dark to stay

Should I fall and be absorbed
Into a different dimension of life?
Or should I fight and jettison cargo
To stay closer to the light?

I know I'm entirely projecting
My vision of good onto someone who's stayed
Sucked in because I took a low orbit
Rather than speeding on my way

I didn't believe in black holes
Thought nothing could pull so strong & true
I didn't believe in black holes,
At least until I met you

Glibly By

I realise my whole life
I've been taught a lie
For the world passes
Me glibly by

That truth is elsewhere
I'm on the side
As the world passes
Me glibly by

I finally discover
My purpose and why
And the world passes
Me glibly by

Or I really uncover
My skills and I try
But the world passed
Me glibly by

Mystic

If I cannot have

Magic in my world

Simple truth that tells the tale

Of why all things have gone absurd

Then I must have a world

Where beauty is in everything

Or is in nothing at all

My eyes tell me that it is so

For fast the sirens call

Assurance of Salvation

I don't pretend to know it all
In fact I wish I could
Just throw it all in someone's hands
And find them someone good

I don't pretend to think I'm right
I'm actually mostly wrong
But I don't know about what or when
Until the moment's is gone

But if there really is someone
Around the coming bend
They know the curve and know my world
They know I need a friend

Breadcrumbs

I followed the breadcrumbs and they led me there.

A field that was open.

Silent.

Bare.

A word from the heavens would bring me such joys

Pure.

And distilled.

From human noise.

But now that I'm here I'll dance till I pass.

Watching the stars, while I lay on the grass

OH, HELLO AGAIN

Ichtus

The water I breathe

And can't do without

A fish about water

Has no fear of doubt

And if I don't know

Don't know that you're there

It makes no real difference

For you are my air

Purpose

I purpose therefore I am
I conjure out of the nothingness
A call that wasn't there
My eyes see the world as light and shadow
But a bat's ears perceive it as more
So I will draw some meaning forth
Pull a rabbit from my hat
And create purpose from the void

If there is a God
Then she is my inspiration and guide
A creator who crafted everything
Made nothingness come alive

Mining deep,
I too
the deepest reach
To craft my crumbling human shape
Into a beating soul

My Dream

There it is

I feel it

It calls me again

A whisper

A way

Oh it calls me

away

up again

My dream

is that something

is tapping

at my door

that I will be

alive again

that I will live

to die once more

Angel

I would never have dreamed
That an angel would come
and fuck the devils out of me

But there you were
standing next to your car
looking for something else

But I found you instead.
And you found me
With my hardened tree

As a perfect,
Angelic explorer

Epilogue

I said to my soul

You must now no longer

Ever, forever

Drink again from that cup

But then I found it

Flowing in the streets

and that same wine again

the sweetness I'd forbidden

sweetest that my lips ever touched

(could it not restrain?)

I broke my vow

Or broke it not

No, I simply died

Reborn yet again in God's love

Shoes Carefully

Lots of shoes
Lots of fancy shoes
Shoes for my blue suit
Shoes for my red one
Lots of shoes in all of the stores
Lots of shoes is good

Good for the shoemakers
Good for the leather makers
Good for the sole makers
Good for the string makers
Only bad for the fathers
Mothers
Daughters
Sons
Children always walking
In lonely shoes
While their parents work for more
Grandchildren always wearing shoes
Because the ground is too hot
Too hot and dry
For anything else

Shoes....
I just bought some shoes

Seeped Me

I wonder if the great beyond
Is just waiting to seep in
Yet
Not as a lightning bolt
But as a wisp of wind
With constant steady rumble
That our ears could never hear
But sometimes in the darkest nights
Its echo floats us near

This hope is but my scratching
Of an itch I think I feel
Even if all is just illusion
Then at least the itch is real

Breather

If I could learn a language
Then it would be your breath
Which fills your form with life
Of the perfect beauty you possess

Each fluttering draw
Each tiny sigh
The way it pauses and starts again--
I want to know, why?

Is there a special hold of your hand
That will keep the rhythm strong
A touch I can place
To make you feel that you belong

Can I help you in some way
To exhale the hurt you bear
And draw in the wonder
That I feel when your body's near

Too deep I maybe venture
Into a life that is not mine
But stronger too is my love of living
To not be awed by your body's rhyme

Raptured Alive

The rapture of living
the bat of an eye
the coo of your lover
the call of the sky
erotic
soothing
nerdy
divine
All the same; neurons
all the same mind
everything sacred
every actsin

Busfenski

She sees the world
As a gift shop of delights
Free for the taking
Enjoyment the only price

The colour of a wall
The dawn of the moon
A fence made of skis
A house with too much room

Boredom is an illusion
Because silence is on her side
Life is breath and breath is living
For she faces the hurt inside

Oh, hello again

pain and pleasure
these two are my guides
whatever the weather
there is nothing better
I'm ever a debtor
yes hopelessly fettered
oh pain
oh pleasure

Definary

Words: sounds that help us understand the past to predict the future.

Mental Health Crisis: The gap between human brains which runs on fractal, complex math with iterative rewards, and an economic system that operates on outdated linear path dependency.

Fly test: don't have a strategy that you wouldn't want to develop if your customer was a fly on the wall.

Gizus Ruler: Is your message so clear and impactful that it is more dangerous if you are dead than if you are alive.

Pun: an intelligence leak due to unused brain capacity and the excessive boringness of most human speech, also known as a word in quantum state.

Hipster: formally competitor in the competition to be most the authentic and eclectic person playing the same game as everyone else

Marketing: becoming the easiest person to ask for the work you want to do.

Museum: walking around 10 minutes of Google, except there are slightly less ads.

Heartbreak: The beautiful sunset of love.

The devil: a comforting explanation to those who want great things, but just can't seem to get them, and are terrified of a chaotic system.

LinkedIn: that place you go to find workaholic friends when nothing else is working to get you a job.

Freedom: choosing what rules to follow

Cynic: A person who enjoys life, but then walks through a dark tunnel and gets scared. Afterwards they keeps their eyes closed so as not to have the shock of darkness reach them again even though the tunnel is long gone.

Facts: the sticks we use to beat people into loving our ideas, even though we really want them to love us.

Art: a key we use to open the beauty of the world around us. A world we're usually too busy to see.

Academia: the place you should go to taste-test a wider variety of BS than is available in normal life.

Student Life

At times we all run like turtles
Slow and groggy for each day
Then there exists blessed coffee
To keep us moving on the way

But more often I run like a squirrel
Fast and frantic; a useless stray
For my health I must find a redder drink
The kind that slurs the words I say

Meaning of Life

Mirror.

Of a monumental kind.

Mimicking the greatest mystery.

Anyone can ever find.

Just as all was drawn from naught.

In a singular moment at an infinite spot.

There banged in an instant all that we know.

From chaos or nothing we can't truly show.

But now we are here.

By some divine magic

You now exist

And the universe itself.

Has given us honour

As a sentient species,

so rare

To build with confidence the life you want
There is a larger story
You reflect the magic of singularity
When you, like the cosmos,
Forge purpose from chaos
Like gold forged deep from exploding stars

Orgas

Life is a cross between bingo and a slot machine.

We are the numbered balls

the funky shapes trying to fall in line.

Love is reaching out grasping,

stepping into the dark and finding close,

those that form our rowdy bunch

Ding ding ding ding, bingo!

All the winners take it all.

You just hit the jackpot.

Cornerstone

My parents gave it early to me
The jewel that they had found
Even before I had left the womb
They spoke it to my soul
"Fearfully and wonderfully made"
And I saw the stone for what it was—
Priceless

I grasped and held it firm
Close upon my chest
Hoping against hope
That it would find its way
Deep into my heart

Many tried to pry it from
My feeble, but growing hands
Or so it felt to me
But I did not give them ground
The Rock was all I could ever be
All I had ever found

Yet precious as it was
It somehow managed to slide
To squirm
or dance
it found somehow
Itself from my grasp

To
To what I do not know
But what I held closely grasped
Grew within my palm
And now I carry with an open hand
Greater weight than I could
Have ever even planned

P.S. 139

O Lord, you have searched me and known me!

You know when I sit down and when I rise up;

you discern my thoughts from afar.

You search out my path and my lying down

and are acquainted with all my ways.

Even before a word is on my tongue,

behold, O Lord, you know it altogether.

You hem me in, behind and before,

and lay your hand upon me.

Such knowledge is too wonderful for me;

it is high; I cannot attain it.

Where shall I go from your Spirit?

Or where shall I flee from your presence?

If I ascend to heaven, you are there!

If I make my bed in Sheol, you are there!

If I take the wings of the morning

and dwell in the uttermost parts of the sea,

even there your hand shall lead me,

and your right hand shall hold me.

If I say, "Surely the darkness shall cover me,

and the light about me be night,"

even the darkness is not dark to you;

the night is bright as the day,

for darkness is as light with you.

For you formed my inward parts;

you knitted me together in my mother's womb.

I praise you, for I am fearfully and wonderfully made.

Wonderful are your works;

my soul knows it very well.

My frame was not hidden from you,

when I was being made in secret,

intricately woven in the depths of the earth.

Your eyes saw my unformed substance;

in your book were written, every one of them,

the days that were formed for me,

when as yet there was none of them.

How precious to me are your thoughts, O God!

How vast is the sum of them!

If I would count them, they are more than the sand.

I awake, and I am still with you.

Oh that you would slay the wicked, O God!

O men of blood, depart from me!

They speak against you with malicious intent;

your enemies take your name in vain.

Do I not hate those who hate you, O Lord?

And do I not loathe those who rise up against you?

I hate them with complete hatred;

I count them my enemies.

Search me, O God, and know my heart!

Try me and know my thoughts!

And see if there be any grievous way in me,

and lead me in the way everlasting!

By An Outcast Shepard Boy

Psalm 139 ESV

Manufactured by Amazon.ca
Bolton, ON